The Morning of the World

Written *by* Bob Hartman
Illustrated *by* Michael McGuire

For Kari, who takes care of the animals. B.H.

To Darlene with love as my best friend and partner. M.M.

VICTOR BOOKS
A Division of Scripture Press Publications Inc.

What was it like, on the morning of the world?

It was clean.

Clean as a baby, fresh from its bath.

Clean as the tires on a brand-new bike.

Clean as a spring sunrise.

Clean as a midnight snowfall.

The first man, Adam, knew nothing about spring,

or snowfall,

or babies,

or bicycles.

But he knew about clean.

He walked on clean soil, and

brushed past clean bushes,

and sniffed clean flowers.

He filled his lungs with clean air,
and his mouth with clean water,
and his belly with the cleanest,
freshest berries anyone has ever tasted.
What was it like, on the morning of the world?
It was clean.

What was it like, on the morning of the world?
It was quiet.
Every now and then, the breeze would catch
hold of a leaf and send it crashing against
its neighbor. Or a stream would bubble
and bounce against its banks. Or the first
man, Adam, would brush against a black-
berry bush or a holly bush or some other
kind of prickly bush, and surprise himself
with a yowp or a yowl.
But, otherwise, it was quiet.
Quiet as a sleeping baby.
Quiet as a coasting bicycle.
Quiet as falling snow.
Quiet as the rising sun.
What was it like, on the morning of the world?
It was quiet. Maybe too quiet.

What was it like, on the morning of the world?
It was time to make some noise.
So God spoke—that was the first noise.

And a zoo of noises followed.
Chirping insects.
Splashing fish.
Singing birds.
Roaring beasts.

Then God said to the first man, Adam,
"Now it's your turn to make some noise!"
And God gave Adam a job.
The best kind of job there is.
A job that is more like a game.

And the game was called,
"Name the Animals."
What was it like, on the morning of the world?
It was time to make some noise.

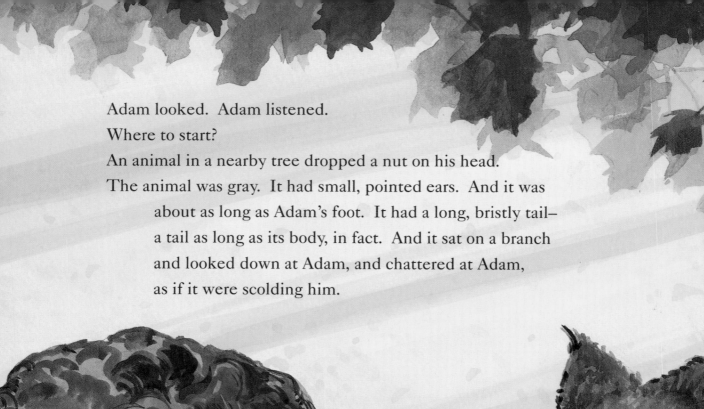

Adam looked. Adam listened.

Where to start?

An animal in a nearby tree dropped a nut on his head.

The animal was gray. It had small, pointed ears. And it was
about as long as Adam's foot. It had a long, bristly tail—
a tail as long as its body, in fact. And it sat on a branch
and looked down at Adam, and chattered at Adam,
as if it were scolding him.

What did Adam name it?

Nobody knows.

But when people who lived in Greece first saw it

and noticed that its tail was as long

and as wide as its body,

they called it "skiouros,"

which means "shadow tail."

What would you have called this gray,

chattering shadow tail

if you were Adam,

on the morning of the world?

Again Adam looked. And again Adam listened.
And Adam spotted another animal shuffling toward him,
    through the undergrowth.
The animal was half as tall as Adam. It was covered with
    bright orange fur. It walked on its feet, like Adam did.
    And on its knuckles, like Adam didn't.

But the most remarkable thing about this animal was its
face–a face that looked a bit like a man's face.
A sad clown face.
What did Adam name it?
Nobody knows.
But when people who lived in Malaysia first saw this animal,
walking through the jungle with its sad clown face,
they called it "orangutan," which means
"man of the woods."
What would you have called it, if you were Adam,
on the morning of the world?

Once more, Adam looked. Once more, Adam listened.
And he heard a munching, crunching sound.
Adam turned around, and right behind him there stood a creature twice
his height, chewing the bark off a tree. It was shaggy and brown.
It had four long, knobby legs. And sticking out of its head were
two branches, like a pair of open hands.
What did Adam name it?
Nobody knows.
But when the people who lived in North America first saw
this huge, shaggy animal, they called it "moos,"
which means "he strips off bark."
What would you have named it, if you were Adam,
on the morning of the world?
So Adam named the animals.
Nobody knows what he called them.
Nobody knows how long it took.

But when he was finished,
     Adam looked at the world.
And he saw that it was no longer clean.
The trees were full of birds' nests.
The ground was punctured with rabbit holes.
The streams were littered with fish.
And there was hardly a leaf, anywhere,
     that hadn't been chewed
     or chomped or nibbled on.
Then Adam listened to the world.
And he heard that it was no longer quiet.
The air was full of cawing and squawking and singing.
The ground was crawling with snorting
     and grunting and squeaking.
The streams were ringing with jumping
     and splashing and diving.
And the jungle rustled and snapped and shook.
What was it like, on the morning of the world?
It was no longer quiet and clean.
It was noisy. It was a mess.
So God gave Adam a name for it.

And the name God gave
it was "Good."

Other books in this series are:
The Edge of the River (the story of baby Moses and his sister Miriam)
The Middle of the Night (the story of young Samuel called by God)
The Birthday of a King (the story of the birth of Jesus)

The story you have just read is based on the second chapter of Genesis.
We encourage you to read the Bible passage itself and
discover even more about God's wonderful Word.

Art direction: Paul Higdon/Grace K. Chan Mallette
Production: Myrna Hasse
Editing: Liz Morton Duckworth

ISBN: 1-56476-040-5

1 2 3 4 5 6 7 8 9 10 Printing/Year 97 96 95 94 93

VICTOR BOOKS
A division of SP Publications, Inc.
Wheaton, Illinois 60187